YOUR KNOWLEDGE HAS VALUE

Portfolio Insurance and VaRoP. A Comparison

Ralf Hohmann

Bibliographic information published by the German National Library:

The German National Library lists this publication in the National Bibliography; detailed bibliographic data are available on the Internet at http://dnb.dnb.de.

ISBN: 9783346408693
This book is also available as an ebook.

© GRIN Publishing GmbH
Nymphenburger Straße 86
80636 München

Print and binding: Books on Demand GmbH, Norderstedt, Germany
Printed on acid-free paper from responsible sources.

The present work has been carefully prepared. Nevertheless, authors and publishers do not incur liability for the correctness of information, notes, links and advice as well as any printing errors.

GRIN web shop: https://www.grin.com/document/1012495

Portfolio insurance and VaRoP - a comparison

Contents

Introduction

Investments in money and capital markets involve different loss potentials that market participants should be able to manage. Below is an overview and comparison of selected strategies to manage the risks.

Portfolio insurance (PI) strategies were developed in the 1980s. They are used to hedge portfolios or individual investments against price losses. The volume of assets hedged with these strategies is significant. Different forms of individual strategies have developed over the years.

Risk quantification and Value at Risk (VAR) strategies emerged around the same time. Risks of individual investments or portfolios were measured and different strategies were developed to take them into account in Value at Risk optimised portfolios (VaRoP). VaRoP is a strategy that calculates an optimal portfolio taking into account a given or permissible maximum VAR.

Both strategies are intended to protect portfolios from losses in value. Their similarities and differences are presented and summarised in this paper. Their applicability in practice is also examined.

Portfolio Insurance

Portfolio insurance is a form of programme trading, like block trading and index arbitrage. In block trading, market participants can offer extensive positions in individual assets or entire portfolios to a block trader without having to look for special counterparties. In index arbitrage, on the other hand, market participants exploit deviations of an index future or an index option from the respective theoretical values. With suitable transactions, they can then achieve almost risk-free excess returns on the spot or futures market.

The literature provides a variety of definitions for portfolio insurance.[1] Summarising these, the aim is to protect a portfolio against losses in value. This protection can cover the whole or parts of the portfolio. It regularly consists of interest-bearing financial securities, stocks and futures market instruments. To protect the portfolio, market participants reduce the amount of stocks if the portfolio value approaches the minimum value set ex ante in the event of price losses. At the same time, they increase the amount of interest-bearing financial securities. Conversely, market participants proceed when the portfolio's price increases. Portfolio insurance strategies follow predefined trading rules; there is no demand for forecasting future developments. They provide protection against systematic capital market risks and can be used for any form of capital investment with a risk premium.[2] The main strategies of portfolio insurance are the stop-loss strategy, the synthetic put strategy and the constant proportion strategy.

---

[1] See T. Ebertz and C. Schlenger, 5/1995. R. Hohmann, 1996, pp. 12-16.
[2] R. Uhlmann, 2008, p. 3 and 17.

Stop-loss strategy

In the stop-loss strategy (SLS), market participants specify ex ante a minimum price below which the value of the portfolio or the stocks should not fall until the end of the investment period.[3] If the value reaches the stop-loss price, the portfolio or the stocks are sold and the funds received are invested in risk-free interest-bearing securities. In a dynamic stop-loss strategy, the portfolio or the stocks are bought back if the corresponding values rise above the stop-loss price again. If the stop-loss price rises as the level of the risk-free interest rate during the investment period, then market participants realise a comparable return at the end of the investment period. They also maintain their participation in increases in the value of the portfolio or individual stocks. In practice, it has been shown that this strategy leads to the desired result.[4]

Synthetic put strategy

In the synthetic put strategy (SPI), market participants use long and short positions in stocks and interest-bearing financial securities. In this way, they can generate a theoretical value trend and the resulting cash flows of a put option. They use money market securities or medium-term investments, as well as etocks or entire portfolios for this purpose. The positions to be taken are derived from the option valuation theory according to the binomial model or the formula of Black and Scholes[5]. Formula 1 is as follows:

Formula 1: Put-call parity for option valuation:

$$P_t = C_t + K*(1+r_f)^{-(T-t)} -S_t$$

with: P_t = price of the put in t
     C_t = Price of the call in t
     $K*(1+r_f)^{-(T-t)}$ = exercise price of the option discounted with rf   for   the   remaining term (T-t)
     r_f = risk-free interest (rate)
     S_t = (base) price (of the portfolio) in t

Market participants can duplicate the value of an option. To do this, they take a long position in t in the amount of C_t, a short position in the amount of -St and a discounted long position in the amount of $K*(1+r_f)^{-(T-t)}$ in order to have built up the theoretical price of a put option with a long position in P_t. These positions must be continuously adjusted to changing market conditions and timing during the hedging period. At the end of the investment period, market participants hold a position in a portfolio that is synthetically hedged with a put option. Synthetic put strategies are easy to illustrate in theory. They should also be easy to apply in practice, especially for institutional market participants. Nevertheless, they have not been used to any significant extent in recent years. The reasons for this are not apparent; any obstacles to increased use presumably need to be removed.

---

[3] See K. Quandt, 2-3.8.2002.
[4] However, increased transaction costs due to more frequent adjustments of the portfolio have a negative effect. Problems also arise in the event of sudden, very pronounced price changes, such as a "flash crash". This also applies to other forms of portfolio insurance. See R. Benders and M. Maisch, 24.11.2009. R. Benders and M. Eberle, 10.5.2010. U. Rettberg, 10.5.2010. T. Riecke, 1.3.2007. O.V., 22.4.2015. B. Finke, 23.4.2015. K. Slodcyk and A. Dörner, 23.4.2015. C. Siedenbiedel, 24.4.2015.
[5] On option pricing, see F. Black and M. Scholes, 1973, pp. 637-654. J. C. Cox and S. A. Ross, 1976, pp. 145-166. L. Jurgeit, 1989.

Constant-Proportion-Portfolio-Insurance

In constant proportion portfolio insurance (CPPI) for stocks or other forms of investment, market participants specify a minimum value for the portfolio. This minimum value is the floor and is smaller than the portfolio value in $t = 0$. The floor increases by a certain percentage during the hedging period.[6]

The difference between the portfolio value and the floor is the cushion. This value is variable and results from the dynamic adjustment of the portfolio from formula 2:

Formula 2: Exposure of Constant Proportion Portfolio Insurance

$E_t = m * Q_t$, and $Q_t = V_t - G_t$, $0 < G_t$

with: E_t = Exposure in t
  m = multiplier
  Q_t = Cushion in t
  V_t = Value of the hedged portfolio in t
  G_t = Floor in t

The exposure E_t is the proportion of the portfolio in risky securities.[7]

If the value of the portfolio increases and $E_t > E_{t-1}$, then the shares of the risky positions are expanded according to formula 2. Here, stocks are bought and interest-bearing securities, ideally zero-coupon bonds, are sold.

In the event of price losses of the portfolio and/or increases in the value of the floor, if $E_t < E_{t-1}$, the risky positions are reduced accordingly. Stocks are sold and interest-bearing securities, at best zero-coupon bonds, are bought.

At the end of the investment period, the value of the portfolio is assumed to be at least equal to the floor. The[8] probability of losses of the portfolio is thus reduced to zero. The probability of increases in the value of the hedged portfolio is maintained.[9]

The multiplier has a special theoretical meaning, as formula 2 shows. The larger the multiplier, the more extensive the purchases and sales, the more the composition of the portfolio changes.[10]

---

[6] For example, around the interest rate for risk-free investments, here the interest rate for risk-free zero-coupon bonds with a comparable maturity. See also R. Uhlmann, 2008, pp. 31-32.
[7] Risky securities here are accordingly stocks or also futures and options. See R. Hohmann, 1996, pp. 105-109 and the sources cited there.
[8] If short sales are not permitted, E_t can be represented as follows: $E_t = \max [m^*Q_t ; 0]$
If borrowing is prohibited, formula 2 for determining E_t is accordingly: $E_t = \min[m^*(V_t - G_t) ; S_t]$
If the floor is known ex ante, the portfolio value can be represented as follows: $V_t = \max [G_t ; G_t + Q_t]$
[9] This is the difference to a comprehensive hedge with futures, where the probability of participating in later price increases of the portfolio is partially or completely given up.
[10] One way to determine the multiplier is for market participants to set the level of the multiplier ex ante. Then they determine the amount of the initial exposure or floor depending on the portfolio value. Then $m = (E_t / G_t)$. See R. Hohmann, 1996, p. 109. R. Uhlmann, 2008, pp. 38-41.

A suitable multiplier is essential if the portfolio value in T is to be above that of the floor. It seems obvious that with inappropriately large multipliers, the losses of exposure as a result of price jumps can be so great that they can no longer be compensated for by increases in the value of the interest-bearing securities. [11, 12]

VAR and VaRoP

The Value at Risk (VAR) measure shows the maximum loss that market participants can theoretically realise for a defined time horizon with a given confidence interval and standard deviation of their risk position.[13] Risk positions can be stocks, interest-bearing securities, derivatives or entire portfolios thereof.

Market participants first determine the size and standard deviation of their risk position. They determine the degree of certainty for the confidence interval, e.g. 95% or 99% certainty.[14] They also assume a certain probability distribution, usually the normal distribution. The time horizon must also be determined, usually from one day to one year. The market participants can then calculate the VAR.[15]

Essential to the calculation of VAR is the estimation of volatility. It can be determined in different ways, e.g. from historical data, via simulations or calculations of the implied volatility of options.[16]

The VAR is calculated using the formula 3.

Formula 3: Calculation VAR

$$VAR = V_t * \sigma * Confid * (T-t) * \sqrt{(T-t)/250}$$

The procedure for calculating the daily VAR for a theoretical equity portfolio is illustrated with an example.[17] The individual values required are:

Portfolio value Vt = 1 Mio
Confidence level 95% = 1.6448
Portfolio variance σ^2 = 0.0165

---

[11] See A. F. Perold, 1986, p. 7. S. Mantel, 2014, pp. 42-43.
[12] There is therefore a suggestion in the literature that the multiplier should not be greater than the reciprocal of the amount of the largest expected negative price jump. See R. Uhlmann, 2008, pp. 136-139, 143. Another interesting question here is whether the multiplier should be determined with the help of the maximum sustainable value at risk. This question cannot be answered here. See the other sections of this paper.
[13] See B Jendruschewitz, 1997, pp. 6-7. P Jorion, 2002, pp. 22-25, 117. For different forms of risk, see ibid, 2002, pp. 15-21. M Choudhry, 2006, pp. 30-32. For definition and differentiation of risks, see ibid, pp. 3-7. For different quantitative measurements of risks, see ibid, pp. 9-11.
[14] For the determination of the confidence interval, see B. Jendruschewitz, 1997, pp. 19, 32. M. Choudhry, 2006, pp. 23, 46-47.
[15] The expected loss associated with an intercept below the normal distribution curve and the critical confidence interval, in relation to the defined time horizon and the calculated standard deviation, see B. Jendruschewitz, 1997, pp. 19-20, 26-29. M. Choudhry, 2006, pp. 24-26, 35-36, 51-52.
[16] On this see B. Jendruschewitz, 1997, pp. 31-32, 35-37, 39-40, 50-61, 64-73.
[17] See T.M. Guldiman, 1995. B Jandruschewitz, 1997, pp. 20, 30, 33, 36-39, 96-100. P. Jorion, 2002, pp. 108-113.

Portfolio Standard Deviation σ12,848%
95% standard deviation 1.6448
VAR = 1 million * 12.848 * 1.6448 * $\sqrt{1/250}$

$\Rightarrow$ VAR = 0.2113 m

If the VAR is to be calculated for several combined positions, then the[18] matrix calculation is suitable.

Volatilities and standard deviations change continuously. To assess the risk, market participants should also continuously calculate the respective VAR of the portfolio.[19]

VAR alone is not active management. It must be embedded in an extended management strategy[20], in this case the Value at Risk optimised Portfolio (VaRoP) strategy.

In VaRoP strategies, market participants first define their risk positions across all forms of investment. To do this, they calculate the VAR of the total position using formula 3.

They then determine their optimal portfolio, derived from portfolio theory[21] and via Efficient Market Theory (EMT) and the capital market line.[22] Given a risk-free interest rate, the market participants can then calculate the efficient capital market curve. This shows the maximum expected return for a portfolio composition at a given risk. Simplified, the procedure via VaRoP can be formally represented as follows:

If VAR $V_0 \leq$; $VAR_t = S_t$, $V_t - S_t = B_{rf}$
If VAR > V_0; $VAR_t = V_0$, $B_{rf} = 0$.

with B = Bond / Bond to rf

In t + 1 these steps are to be repeated.

In t_0, the market participants determine their optimal portfolio according to the EMT. At the same time, they calculate the VAR of this position. If the efficient portfolio is at or within an admissible risk range, no transactions are executed. However, if the portfolio is outside the permissible portfolio range, then the market participants adjust it through corresponding transactions. Since the determinants change regularly over time, continuous buying and selling transactions can be expected.

---

[18] On matrix accounting, see L. Kruschwitz, 1995, p. 314. See also B. Jendruschewitz, 1997, pp. 31, 34, 45-47, 78-80. M.Choudhry, 2006, pp. 39-44.
[19] For a summary and critique of the VAR, see B. Jendruschewitz, 1997, pp. 110-112.
[20] On divergent risk management via limits, see B. Jendruschewitz, 1997, pp. 20-22. On VAR for active risk management, see P. Jorion, 2002, pp. 383-387.
On VAR for interest bearing financial instruments see M. Choudhry, 2006, pp. 62-86, for options see ibid, pp. 88-99, for Monte Carlo simulations see ibid, pp. 102-107.
[21] See H.M. Markowitz, 1952, pp. 77-91. The same, 1970. L. Perridon, M. Steiner and A. Rathgeber, 2009, pp. 252-258. J. Berk and P. DeMarzo, 2017, pp. 401-409.
[22] L. Perridon, M. Steiner and A. Rathgeber, 2009, pp. 263-267. J. Berk and P. DeMarzo, 2017, pp. 417-422.

Comparison

Stop Loss and VAR / VaRoP

In the stop-loss strategy (SLS), the floor is subtracted from the assets V_t. This results in the position S_t to be invested in risky securities. S_t is greater than zero, or S_t is equal to zero. Formally represented as follows: V_t - Floor = S_t, with $S_t > 0$; S_t; 0

The risky asset s_t takes on this role in comparison with the VAR, without forecasts of volatility and without active management of the position S_t. There is only a steady adjustment of the size of S_t, according to the changes in V_t - Floor = S_t.

S_t is only similar to VaRoP with active management of the portfolio V_t. Here, a forecast of the volatility and an anticipatory adjustment of the portfolio is made, corresponding to the procedures of strategies with VaRoP. Formally, it can be represented as follows:

S_t = VAR without management
= VaRoP with management (combination of passive strategies with volatility forecast)

=> V_t VaRoP≈, S_t ≈ VAR
=> V_t - VAR ≈ VaRoP
=> VaRoP - VAR ≈ r_f ≈ Bond ≈ Floor * r_f

Synthetic Put and VAR / VaRoP

The put-call strategy is decisive for strategies with a synthetic put (SPS). It formally reads:

$P - C = K * (1-r_f)^{(T-t)} - S_t$

Here S_t is to be compared with VaRoP. P should correspond to VAR, and S_t minus the discounted strike price of the option can also correspond to VAR. Also, the strike price of the option should take values of the floor. Formally, it is as follows:

=> S_t ≈ VaRoP
=> P ≈ VAR
=> $S_t - K * (1-r_f)^{(T-t)}$ ≈ VAR
=> C ≈ r_f (C ≈ Floor)

CPPI and VAR / VaRoP

Formula 2 is crucial for constant proportion portfolio insurance (CPPI) strategies. It reads:

$E_t = m * Q_t$, and $Q_t = V_t - G_t, 0 < G_t$

Here, the comparison shows that E comes close to the actively adjusted part VaRoP.[23]

$\Rightarrow E \approx VaRoP$
$\Rightarrow VaRoP - VAR \approx Floor$
$\Rightarrow 1/VAR = min. floor$

Also, the multiplier can be used to select the confidence interval.

$\Rightarrow m \approx Confid.$

Similarities, differences and combination of SLS, SPS, CPPI and VaRoP seem obvious. In simplified terms, these can be expressed as follows:

$V_t \approx VaRoP, S_t \approx VaRoP, E \approx VaRoP$

What all strategies have in common is that risks are controlled and that risk positions and the amount of risk are to be determined beforehand. Portfolios usually consist of risky and risk-free components. The trigger for adjustment varies, as does the management of the portfolio in the event of risk changes. Strike prices and stop-loss limits are comparable.

A comparison shows that the similarities between the strategies outweigh the differences. The facts are the same despite different definitions. However, market participants decide for themselves which aspects are important to them.

The similarities and differences can be presented in a table.

---

[23] See also P. Jorion, 2002, pp. 384-387.

Table 1. Differences and similarities of the strategies

	SLS	SPS	CPPI	VaRoP
Risk definition		√	(√)	√
Risk scope	√	√	√	√
Risk position	√	√	√	√
Risky shares	√	√	√	√
Risk-free units/ Floor/ Basis	√	√	√	√
Forecast? Distribution assumption		√		√
Trigger adjustment	√	√	√	√
Management Risky shares		√	√	√
Portfolio theory, EMT relevant		√		√
VAR or VaRoP to determine floor				√
Base price, SL limits	√	√	√	√

Summary and outlook

The various forms of portfolio insurance are suitable for protecting portfolios against losses in value. Value At Risk describes the maximum loss to be expected from a position. VaRoP shows how positions are to be optimised under consideration of a permissible VAR. Portfolio insurance and VaRoP show similarities and also deal with different aspects.

It is to be expected that all strategies will continue to be essential for the management of portfolios in the future. What is interesting here is how the still little-known strategies of VaRoP find their way into daily business. This development would not be unjustified. It is exciting to follow this further.

Appendix: Assumptions and discussion

For the strategies of portfolio insurance and VaRoP, some ideal-typical assumptions on German money and capital markets are assumed.[24] These are then to be examined for their realism.

1. There are arbitrage-free markets. Stocks, stock-index futures and irredeemable credit-risk-free interest-bearing financial instruments are issued and traded simultaneously. In the market, transactions are to be fulfilled immediately.
2. Market access restrictions, transaction costs, taxes, rules or regulations do not exist. Short selling is permitted, short sellers and option writers fulfil their obligations.
3. Market participants act rationally and want to maximise their benefits. They invest in stocks and index futures as well as credit-risk-free financial securities.
4. Financial securities are divisible at will.
5. Dividend payments and capital increases or decreases do not take place.
6. Only one currency exists. The borrowing and investment of financial resources for any period is always possible at the interest rate on credit risk-free assets. This risk-free interest rate is positive, known and constant during the hedging period. The yield curve is horizontal.
a) Stock prices follow a multiplicative binomial process over equidistant periods with known and constant probability of possible returns over each period.
b) Stock prices have a steady course and trading on the markets takes place continuously. The distribution of expected returns for a diversified equity portfolio is log-normally distributed at the end of a time interval. The volatility of stock prices is constant and known throughout the time horizon.

Discussion of assumptions

The examples of portfolio insurance strategies in the previous part have the assumptions made above as a precondition. For the practical application, it must be checked whether the assumptions correspond to the conditions in reality. Any deviations that occur must be investigated and their effects on the strategies determined as well as alternative solutions named.[25]

According to assumption 1, simultaneous trading can always take place when prices are established on the cash market. As a rule, liquidity in the market is greatest around noon. Markets in reality always give the opportunity for arbitrage[26] and some trades on the spot and futures market do not have to be fulfilled immediately.[27] However, this circumstance can be planned for. Deviations from the theoretically correct prices can be determined by market participants themselves, and delivery deadlines can be integrated into strategies. However, under certain circumstances, the strategies can have an influence on the price developments on the cash and derivatives markets.[28]

---

[24] Cf. R. Hohmann, 1996, pp. 20-21. On the discussion of assumptions, cf. ibid. pp. 128-250. See also the same. 2015, S. 15.
[25] For a comparable discussion of assumptions, see R. Uhlmann, 2008, pp. 103-4, 120-132.
[26] See R. Hohmann, 1991. The same, 1996, pp. 220-226. The same, 2015, p. 59.
[27] For trading and delivery regulations in Germany, see www.Xetra and Deutsche Börse/Handelszeiten.com
[28] R. Hohmann, 1996, pp. 225-6 and the sources cited there. R. Uhlmann, 2008, p. 62.

Contrary to assumption 2, in reality there are market entry restrictions for individual investors in selected markets and there are certain rules and regulations that do not need to be discussed conclusively here. However, this is not relevant for the majority of market participants. Transaction costs and taxes also exist. Transaction costs are to be integrated into the strategies ex ante,[29] they then have a negative influence on the result of the strategy. Taxes are incurred ex post, they do not directly influence the feasibility of the strategies. Permitted short sales and option transactions should always be fulfilled in official trading on the futures markets;[30] collateral is not necessary within the framework of the strategy.[31]

Assumption 3 should be correct, even if in the case of price slides followed immediately by price recoveries[32], or in the case of investments in interest-bearing securities with a negative yield instead of, for example, cash hoarding, doubts may arise as to the rationality of market participants.

All financial securities are arbitrarily divisible. Assumption 4 applies when market participants increase the size of their portfolio to the point where they can use a whole unit of a financial security as the smallest unit within their strategy.

Fortunately, contrary to assumption 5, dividend payments and capital increases or decreases occur in reality. They can therefore either be neglected in the context of the strategies and then have a certain influence on the result of the strategy. Or, since they are usually known ex ante, they are integrated into the strategies.

Assumption 6 is applicable if the market participant invests in only one currency. When investing in several currencies, the market participant must then take the corresponding dependencies into account.

Borrowing and investing financial resources is always possible for any period of time at the interest rate on credit-risk-free investments. This circumstance applies to market participants with first-class credit ratings. Others usually have to endure a credit rating discount or premium. This interest rate is assumed to be positive, known and constant during the hedging period. The[33] yield curve is horizontal.

As of 2015, the interest rate is almost no longer positive for securities with a first credit rating, both in Germany and in some other European countries. It is also not always known to all market participants and it is never constant. The yield curve is horizontal in very few cases.[34] Looking at the experience that market participants have gained over the past decades or centuries, it cannot necessarily be assumed that negative interest rates are the norm or that they will exist for long. Unknown interest rates can be replaced by known quantities determined on official markets, constant interest rates can be created via forward rates or very small hedging

---

[29] On transaction costs see R. Hohmann, 1996, pp. 198-217 and the sources cited there. The highest transaction costs are incurred when trading shares on the cash market, the lowest when trading futures on the futures market. For trading filter trading rules, see R. Uhlmann, 2008, pp. 36-7. S. Mantel, 2014, pp. 33-35.

[30] Without the possibility of short selling, constant proportion portfolio insurence would be path-dependent. R. Uhlmann, 2008, p. 51.

[31] Collateral is not necessary here, since Vt=0 = 100% of the market participant's assets. Cash collateral can result in interest losses. Also because of these opportunity losses, collateral should be dispensed with in the following.

[32] For rumours and Fat Finger see o.V., 22.4.2015..

[33] On monetary stability and inflation see R. Hohmann, 1996, p. 130, fn. 3 and 4.

[34] For the yield curve, see for example the statistical supplements to the monthly reports of the Deutsche Bundesbank.

periods.[35] The same applies to the yield curve. These circumstances should be taken into account via formula 2.[36]

According to assumption 7a, stock prices follow a multiplicative binomial process over equidistant periods with known and constant probability of possible returns over each period. This assumption was made in order to be able to represent the course of stock prices within the framework of the binomial model. If one reduces the observation periods to the smallest sizes, then stock prices follow a binomial model with probabilities that should be known in advance and also constant.[37]

According to assumption 7b, stock prices have a steady course and trading on the markets takes place continuously. The distribution of expected returns for a diversified equity portfolio is log-normally distributed at the end of a time interval. The volatility of stock prices is constant and known throughout the time horizon. Stock prices for securities of first credit quality and suitable market depth should have a steady course. Trading should also be continuous during trading hours and also pre- and post-trading. In practice, the distribution of returns for a diversified equity portfolio should be log-normally distributed at the end of a time interval. Deviations during small intervals, such as the crisis after the attacks in 2001, the banking crisis in 2008 and the Brexit crisis in 2016, should be refrained from. The volatility of stock prices is not always known and not constant.[38] This can be countered if the market participant defines the hedging period sufficiently small and then immediately follows it with a chain of new small periods. Also, volatility then has no direct influence on the strategy.[39]

Assumptions 1 to 7 describe the reality in an ideal-typical way. They serve to illustrate the strategies and simplify their understanding. Deviations from reality exist. However, these can either be neglected or circumvented with a few aids. In the following, the assumptions are assumed to be largely valid; no further critical analyses are carried out.

---

[35] It must also be taken into account that the floor can change considerably in the event of unforeseen interest rate jumps. In this case, shorter intervals or scenarios on the probability of the change should be used.

[36] It should be noted that, as a rule, falling interest rates have a positive influence on stock prices. R. Hohmann, 1996, p. 137, fn. 2. Interest rate changes have influences on the prices of futures. This should be reduced if only short-dated futures or single-period strategies are used. On variable interest rates and solutions see R. Hohmann, 1996, pp. 160-168. On interest rate risks in financial securities see H. Schmidt, 1979, p. 711. The same, 198i, p. 74.

[37] See R. Hohmann, 1996, p. 115, fn. 1.

[38] For a review of the literature, see R. Hohmann, 1996, pp. 182-189.

[39] An exception are perhaps lower or more frequent trading transactions with corresponding transaction costs. To adjust the multiplier on volatility with volatility caps see R. Uhlmann, 2008, p. 40. On the advantage of lower historical or actual volatility compared to implied volatility see ibid, p. 50. On the criticism of the assumption of normal distribution see B. Jendruschewitz, 1997, pp. 39-40.

Bibliography

Benders, Rolf, Eberle, Matthias (2010)
Aktiencrash verstört Anleger in den USA, in Handelsblatt, No. 89, 10.5.2010, p. 40.

Benders, Rolf, Maisch, Michael (2009)
Temposünder unter Verdacht, in Handelsblatt, No. 227, 24.11.2009, p. 42.

Berk, Jonathan, DeMarzo, Peter (2017)
Corporate Finance, Harlow, England, 2017.

Black, Fischer, Scholes, Myron (1973)
The pricing of options and corporate liabilities, in Journal of Political Economy, Vol. 81, Nr. 3, 1973, pp. 637-654.

Choudhry, Mourad (2006)
An introduction to value-at-risk, 4. Edition, Chichester, West Sussex, 2006.

Cox, John C., Ross, Stephen. A (1976)
The valuation of options for alternative stochastic processes, in Journal of Financial Economics, Vol. 3, 1976, pp. 145-166.

Ebertz, Thomas, Schlenger, Christian (1995)
Absicherungsstrategien für institutionale Portfolios, in Die Bank, 5/1995, pp. 302-307.

Finke, Björn (2015)
Zocker aus der Doppelhaushälfte, in Süddeutsche Zeitung, No. 93, 23.4.2015, p. 17.

Guldiman, Till M. (1995)
RiskMetrics - Tecknical Dokumant, 3. Edition, 26.5.1995, pp. 26-27.

Hohmann, Ralf (1991)
Der Einfluß der Wertpapierleihe auf die Bewertung des DAX Future, in KaRS Kapitalanlagen, Recht und Steuern, issue 8/9, 1991, pp. 574-582.

Hohmann, Ralf (1996)
Portfolio Insurance in Deutschland, Wiesbaden 1996.

Hohmann, Ralf (2015)
Portfolio Insurance in der Praxis, in Die Bank, No. 5/2015, pp. 13-15.

Jendruschewitz, Boris (1997)
Value at Risk, Ein Ansatz zum Management von Marktrisiken in Banken, Frankfurt am Main, 1997.

Jorion, Philippe (2002)
Value at Risk, The new benchmark for managing risk, 2. Edition, Singapur, 2002.

Jurgeit, Ludwig (1989)
Bewertung von Optionen und bonitätsrisikobehafteten Finanztiteln, Wiesbaden 1989.

Kruschwitz, Lutz (1995)
Investitionsrechnung, Berlin-New York, 1995.

Mantel, Stefan (2014)
Constant Proportion Portfolio Insurance, Duale Hochschule Villingen-Schwenningen, 2014.

Markowitz, Harry Max (1952)
Portfolio Selection, Journal of Finance, 1952, Vol. 7, pp. 349-360.

Markowitz, Harry Max (1970)
Portfolio Selection. Efficient Diversification of Investments, New Haven - London, 1970.

O.V. (2015)
Brite wegen "Flash Crash" an Wall Street fetgenommen, in Die Welt, www. Welt.de, 22.4.2015, pp. 1-3.

Perold, André. F. (1986)
Constant proportion portfolio insurance, Harvard Business School working paper, 1986, S. 7.

Perold, André. F., Sharpe, William F. (1988)
Dynamic strategies for asset allocation, in Financial Analyst Journal, Vol. 44, Nr. 1, 1988, p. 22.

Perridon, Louis, Steiner, Manfred and Rathgeber, Andreas (2009)
Finanzwirtschaft der Unternehmung, Munich, 2009.

Quandt, Kathrin (2002)
Mit Stop-Loss-Marken das Aktiendepot absichern, in Handelsblatt, No. 147, 2.-3.8.2002, p. 34.

Rettberg, Udo (2010)
An der Börse geht es um Nanosekunden, in Handelsblatt, No. 89, 10.5.2010, p. 40.

Riecke, Thorsten (2007)
Die Wall Street atmet auf, in Handelsblatt, No. 43, 1.3.2007, p. 22.

Schmidt, Hartmut (1979)
Liquidität von Finanztiteln als integrierendes Konzept der Bankbetriebslehre, in: Zeitschrift für Betriebswirtschaft, 49. Jg., Heft 8, 1979, p. 711.

Schmidt, Hartmut (1981)
Wertpapierbörsen, in Bank- und Börsenwesen, Vol. 1, Struktur und Leistungsangebot, Ed. Michael Bitz, Munich 1981.

Siedenbiedel, Christian (2015)
Der Mann, der Wall Street in die Knie zwang, in Frankfurter Allgemeine Sonntagszeitung, No. 17, 24.4.2015, p. 33.

Slodcyk, Katharina and Dörner, A. (2015)
Der Crash aus der Vorstadt, in Handelsblatt, No. 78, 23.4.2015, p. 30.

Uhlmann, Roger (2008)
Portfolio Insurance - CPPI im Vergleich mit anderen Strategien, Bern Stuttgart Wien, 2008.

List of abbreviations

as a rule	as a rule
Confid	Confidence interval
CPPI	Constant Proportion Portfolio Insurance
cf.	compare
d	down, downturn, price losses
Ders.	The same
Ed.	Publisher
EMT	Efficient Market Theory
e.g.	for example
ex ante	a priori
Fn.	Footnote
ibid	ibidem
Long	Bought
max	Maximum from
min.	min. / at least
No.	Number
o.V.	without author
PI	Portfolio Insurance
p.	Page
Short	(Empty)sold
SLS	Stop-loss strategy
SPS	Synthetic Put Strategy
u	up, upswing, price gains
VAR	Value At Risk
VaRoP	Value at Risk optimised portfolio
Vol.	Volume

Symbol directory

Br_f	Bond / Bond at r_f
C_t	Price of a European call in t
E_t	value of an exposure in t
F_t	Value of a future in t
G_t	Value of a floor in t
GE	Money unit
K	Exercise price of an option
m	Multiplier
P_t	Price of a European put in t
r	Interest rate
r_f	risk-free interest rate
Q_t	Value of a Cushion in t
S_t	(base) price (of a portfolio, share, bond, currency) in t
T	End point of a temporal series, duration, distance. Time
t	Starting point of a temporal series, duration, distance. Time
V_t	Value of a hedged portfolio, share, bond, currency in t
<	none
>	greater
σ^2	Volatility
σ	Standard deviation
%	Percent